Out and About at the UNITED STATES MINT

by Nancy Garhan Attebury

illustrated by Zachary Trover

Special thanks to our adviser for her expertise:

Susan Kesselring, M.A., Literacy Educator
Rosemount–Apple Valley–Eagan (Minnesota) School District

PICTURE WINDOW BOOKS
Minneapolis, Minnesota

The author wishes to thank Rich, Ramirose, and Garhan Attebury
for their love and support.

Editorial Director: Carol Jones
Managing Editor: Catherine Neitge
Creative Director: Keith Griffin
Editor: Jill Kalz
Story Consultant: Terry Flaherty
Designer: Zachary Trover
Page Production: Picture Window Books
The illustrations in this book were created digitally.

Picture Window Books
5115 Excelsior Boulevard
Suite 232
Minneapolis, MN 55416
877-845-8392
www.picturewindowbooks.com

Printed in the United States of America.

Library of Congress Cataloging-in-Publication Data
Attebury, Nancy Garhan.
Out and about at the United States Mint / by Nancy Garhan Attebury ; illustrated by
Zachary Trover.
p. cm. — (Field trips)
Includes bibliographical references and index.
ISBN 1-4048-1151-6 (hardcover)
1. United States Mint—Juvenile literature. 2. Coins—United States—Juvenile literature.
I. Trover, Zachary, ill. II. Title. III. Field trips (Picture Window Books)
HG457.G37 2006
737.4973—dc22   2005004267

We're going on a field trip to the United States Mint. We can't wait!

Things to find out:

How does the United States Mint get pictures and words on a coin?

Why do coins have raised edges?

What does "in mint condition" mean?

What happens to the coins after they are made?

$AVE

3

Good morning! My name is Sara. Welcome to the United States Mint of Philadelphia. Our job is to make coins, and we make a lot of them! Today you'll see how much work goes into making coins before they get to your pocket.

4

The United States Mint is headquartered in Washington, D.C. Actual coins are made, or minted, in Philadelphia, Pennsylvania, and Denver, Colorado. Paper money is made at the Bureau of Engraving and Printing in Washington, D.C.

5

We'll tour the mint from up here, in the visitors' gallery. For safety and security reasons, no visitors are allowed down by the machinery. We don't want anyone to get hurt. We also want to make sure no one damages the machines.

We make all kinds of coins here. We make pennies, nickels, dimes, quarters, half-dollars, and dollars.

The metal arrives at the mint in huge rolls. If we unrolled one of them, it would be as long as five football fields! Each roll is about 13 inches (33 centimeters) wide and 1,500 feet (450 meters) long.

Pennies are made in a different way. Companies punch out copper-plated zinc penny circles, called blanks, and ship them to the United States Mint so words and pictures can be added to them.

Making coins is a little like making cookies. First, we roll the metal flat like cookie dough by using the machine down below. It's called a blanking press. The press operator guides one end of the metal roll into it. The metal slowly unrolls and goes through the press as a flat sheet.

Next, the machine punches round blanks out of the metal like a cookie cutter cutting shapes out of dough.

After you've cut out your shapes, what do you do with the leftover dough? You make more cookies! Leftover metal is called webbing. It's recycled into more coins.

The United States Mint made its first circulating coin in 1793. Blanks were fed by hand, one at a time, into a machine that stamped words and pictures on them. Imagine how long it took to make money one coin at a time!

The blanks are heated in a red-hot furnace to soften the metal. This step makes it easier to stamp words and pictures on them. The hot blanks are then dropped into a quench tank, where a water and soap mixture cools them.

From the tank, the blanks travel up a whirlaway tube. We call it a "whirlaway" tube because the extra liquid is drained, or "whirled away," through holes in the tube. After the whirlaway tube, blanks are dropped into a giant washing machine, cleaned, and dried.

Furnace temperatures can reach more than 1,500 degrees Fahrenheit (815 degrees Celsius). Cookies are usually baked at one-fourth of that temperature!

Next, the cleaned blanks move to one of our milling machines. These machines raise the rims, or edges, of the blanks. Rims stick up higher than the words or pictures that go on coins later. Rims protect coins from scratches and make them easier to stack.

We've punched out the blanks. We've heated and cooled them. We've washed and dried them and raised their rims. Now, we're finally ready to make these blanks look more like real coins!

Some coins have an edge with little grooves in it. Putting in the grooves is called reeding. This takes place in the stamping press. Quarters, dimes, and half-dollars have reeded edges. Reeding helps identify the different kinds of coins.

These are our stamping presses. Blanks go into a stamping press and come out with words and pictures. Each press is loaded with two steel cylinders called dies. One die, called the anvil, has the words and pictures for the back of the coin. The other die, called the hammer, has the words and pictures for the front. Each press makes just one kind of coin.

The anvil is held still as the hammer hits the blank's surface. If all goes well, each blank leaves the press as a perfect, shiny coin—one that is in "mint condition."

There is a saying that goes, "Heads you win, tails you lose." A flipped coin will land with the head or tail (backside) facing up. At the United States Mint, the coin's head side is called the obverse. The tail side is called the reverse. The phrase should be "Obverse you win, reverse you lose."

New coins fall into a special box called a trap. They are looked at very carefully.

If the coins are the wrong size, have the wrong pictures on them, or have anything else wrong with them, they are scrapped. If the coins are OK, the press operator pulls a lever, and the coins tumble onto a conveyor belt. Their next stop is the counting machines.

A magnifying glass is used to look at each batch of coins. Coins are checked for correct shape and smoothness. If they do not pass, they are sent to the scrap pile and recycled to make new coins.

The counting machines count the coins and drop them into big bags. The bags are sealed shut and carried by forklift to storage vaults.

18

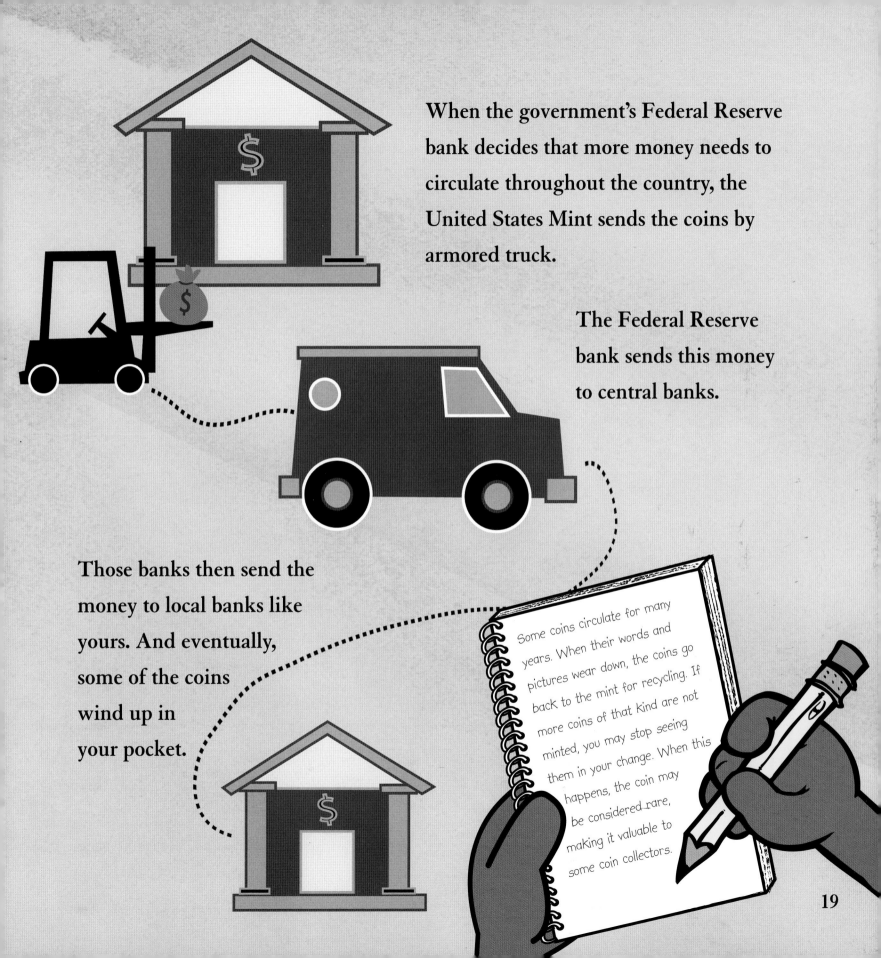

When the government's Federal Reserve bank decides that more money needs to circulate throughout the country, the United States Mint sends the coins by armored truck.

The Federal Reserve bank sends this money to central banks.

Those banks then send the money to local banks like yours. And eventually, some of the coins wind up in your pocket.

Some coins circulate for many years. When their words and pictures wear down, the coins go back to the mint for recycling. If more coins of that kind are not minted, you may stop seeing them in your change. When this happens, the coin may be considered rare, making it valuable to some coin collectors.

The next time you find a shiny, "mint condition" coin, think about all the work it took to make it. Maybe it was made here today during your field trip!

TAKING A CLOSE LOOK AT COINS

You use coins nearly every day, but do you really know what they look like?

What you need:
a penny, a nickel, a quarter, a half-dollar, and a silver dollar
a sheet of white paper, folded in half the long way
a cup you can't see through
a pencil
a marker

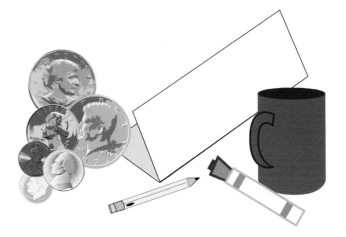

What you do:
1. Drop the coins in the cup.

2. Cover the top with your hand and shake the coins.

3. Take out one coin at a time and study the writing and pictures on each.

4. Put the coins in a row on the top half of the folded paper in order from the smallest value to the largest.

5. Trace around each coin, starting with the penny and moving on to the silver dollar, to create a "blank."

6. Put the coins back in the cup and shake them again.

7. Reach in the cup without looking. Pick one coin at a time. Try to identify the value just by feeling it.

8. Then place each coin between the top and bottom halves of the paper in the right order to match the "blanks" on the top half of your paper.

9. Using the side of a sharpened pencil, gently rub over the first covered coin. Do you see the words and pictures appear on the paper?

10. Repeat these steps with each coin. You may want to make two "blanks"—one for the head (obverse) side and one for the tail (reverse) side.

FUN FACTS

- Before people used money to buy things, they traded for what they wanted. For example, they may have traded an animal skin for a bracelet or sewed clothes in exchange for dental care. Some people today still trade goods or services.

- Each roll of metal used to make coins weighs about 6,000 pounds (2,700 kilograms).

- A mint mark is added to some coins. It tells where the coins were made. Coins made in Philadelphia have a "P" on them, except for the penny. Coins made in Denver have a "D" on them. Coins made in San Francisco have an "S."

- Some presses today can make 750 coins every minute. More than 50 million coins are made, or minted, every 24 hours. The Philadelphia and Denver mints together produce more than 10 billion coins a year. They have produced as many as 27 billion in a single year.

- In 1999, the United States Mint began its 50 State Quarters Program. Through this program, a new quarter is introduced every 10 weeks to honor one of the 50 states. Quarters are introduced in order of the states' "birthdays." Delaware was the first state to have its own quarter because it was the first state to sign the U.S. Constitution. Hawaii will be the last.

GLOSSARY

blanks—round pieces of metal that are ready to be stamped with words and pictures

circulate—to go from one place to another; for example, coins circulate from the United States Mint to the bank and then to you; then when you save up enough of them, you deposit the coins in your bank, or spend them, and the coins continue to circulate

die—a part of the stamping press that has words and/or pictures on it

mint condition—the term given to a new coin that has been freshly made

obverse—the head (front) side of a coin

recycled—used again

reverse—the tail (back) side of a coin

vaults—large safes

webbing—the metal left over after blanks are punched out

TO LEARN MORE

At the Library

Harman, Hollis Page. *Money Sense for Kids!* Hauppauge, N.Y.: Barron's, 2004.

Leedy, Loreen. *Follow the Money!* New York: Holiday House, 2002.

Otfinoski, Steve. *Coin Collecting for Kids*. Norwalk, Conn.: Innovative Kids, 2000.

On the Web

FactHound offers a safe, fun way to find Web sites related to this book. All of the sites on FactHound have been researched by our staff. *www.facthound.com*

1. Visit the FactHound home page.
2. Enter a search word related to this book, or type in this special code: 1404811516.
3. Click on the FETCH IT button.

Your trusty FactHound will fetch the best sites for you!

INDEX

Look for all the books in the Field Trips series:

Out and About at ...

The Apple Orchard
The Aquarium
The Bakery
The Bank
City Hall
The Dairy Farm
The Fire Station
The Hospital
The Newspaper
The Orchestra
The Planetarium
The Post Office
The Public Library
The Science Center
The Supermarket
The United States Mint
The Vet Clinic
The Zoo